Tundra Animals

Connor Dayton

PowerKiDS press
New York

Published in 2009 by The Rosen Publishing Group, Inc.
29 East 21st Street, New York, NY 10010

First Edition

Editor: Nicole Pristash
Book Design: Greg Tucker
Photo Researcher: Jessica Gerweck

Photo Credits: Cover © Getty Images/Maria Stenzel; back cover, pp. 5, 11, 15, 17, 19 Shutterstock.com; p. 7 © Getty Images/George F. Mobley; p. 9 © Getty Images/Yva Momatiuk & John Eastcott; p. 13 © Getty Images/ Steven Kaziowski; p. 21 © Getty Images/Paul Nicklen.

Library of Congress Cataloging-in-Publication Data

Dayton, Connor.
  Tundra animals / Connor Dayton. — 1st ed.
      p. cm. — (American habitats)
  Includes index.
  ISBN 978-1-4358-2768-4 (library binding) — ISBN 978-1-4358-3197-1 (pbk.)
ISBN 978-1-4358-3203-9 (6-pack)
  1. Tundra animals—Alaska—Juvenile literature. I. Title.
  QL161.D396 2009
  591.75'86—dc22
                                        2008039417

Manufactured in the United States of America

Contents

America's Tundra Animals   4

A Cold Climate   6

Tundra Plants   8

Fur and Hooves   10

The Polar Bear   12

Tundra Birds   14

The Snowy Owl   16

Mosquitoes!   18

Freezing Fish   20

Saving Alaska's Tundra   22

Glossary   23

Index   24

Web Sites   24

America's Tundra Animals

Tundra is a **habitat** that is in the northernmost parts of the world. In the United States, tundra is found only in Alaska. The **climate** in this habitat is cold for most of the year.

Animals that live in Alaska's tundra have **adapted** to life in the cold. For example, the arctic fox has fur on the bottoms of its feet and a thick white coat. These things help the arctic fox stay warm. Other tundra animals have adapted like this, too. Put on your coat and get ready to meet some more cool animals of Alaska's tundra!

This arctic fox's white fur allows the fox to hide well in the snow. One animal that hunts arctic foxes is the polar bear.

A Cold Climate

Tundra climate is one of the coldest climates on Earth. In Alaska's tundra, the **temperature** can reach -30° F (-34° C) in the winter! Even in the summer, tundra soil often stays **frozen**. Soil that stays frozen for a long time is called permafrost.

Tundra can also be as dry as a desert! Tundra gets as little as 10 inches (25 cm) of **precipitation** each year. Most of this precipitation is snow. Animals have adapted to living in the snow, though. The snowshoe hare has large, furry feet that help it move quickly over snow and ice without slipping.

When Alaska's tundra is not covered with snow, animals feed on the grasses and plants that grow there, as this herd of caribou is doing.

Tundra Plants

The tundra habitat is so far north that in the winter, the Sun never rises very high in the sky. This means that in the winter, the days are short and the nights are long.

How do tundra plants grow? The mosses, bushes, and grasses that grow in the tundra have **roots** that are not very deep in the ground. This allows the plants to draw in any precipitation that falls. Many tundra plants are small, too, which keeps the plants safe from the blowing wind. These plants are important because many animals feed on them.

Habitat Facts

Some tundra plants, such as the wooly lousewort, grow fur to keep themselves safe from the cold and the wind. This fur is made up of thousands of tiny hairs.

Many brightly colored plants can be seen in Alaska's tundra during the fall.

Mammals can live in cold climates because mammals have fur. Musk oxen are mammals that can live year-round in Alaska's tundra. Musk oxen have long, thick coats. They also have undercoats made of short hairs that keep them extra warm. To find mosses and plant roots to eat, musk oxen have special hooves that help the oxen dig under snow.

Caribou are mammals that are sometimes called reindeer. Caribou spend the summer eating grasses, and then they head south for the winter. A caribou's yearly travels can add up to 1,600 miles (2,575 km)!

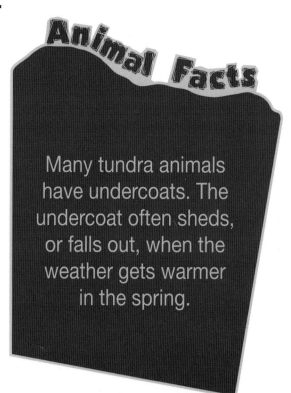

Animal Facts

Many tundra animals have undercoats. The undercoat often sheds, or falls out, when the weather gets warmer in the spring.

This caribou is feeding on some grass. Some adult caribou can eat up to 12 pounds (5 kg) of food every day!

The Polar Bear

Polar bears are mammals that live in the icy, northernmost parts of Alaska's tundra. Like arctic foxes, polar bears have furry feet. Polar bears also have two fur coats to keep warm. A polar bear's skin is black, which draws in heat from the Sun. To keep even warmer, polar bears dig a den in the snow, and they sleep there through part of the long tundra winter.

Polar bears eat walruses, caribou, and other mammals. A polar bear's favorite meal is a seal, which it can smell from 20 miles (32 km) away!

Animal Facts

A polar bear has fat on its body called blubber. Blubber keeps the polar bear warm. Blubber also helps the bear float while it swims!

This mother polar bear (right) and her cub are sitting on Alaska's shore. When the sea turns to ice, the bears will walk on it and look for food.

Tundra Birds

Even though Alaska's tundra air is very cold, birds can still fly and live there. Snow geese often fly over tundra in flocks, which are groups of birds. However, you may hear their loud honks before you see these white, medium-sized birds. Snow geese come to the far northern tundra in the summer to **mate**. Then, they travel south when the weather gets cold.

The arctic tern is another bird that comes to Alaska to mate. When winter comes, arctic terns fly all the way south to Antarctica. This makes the arctic tern quite the traveler!

Arctic terns, like this one, are white, and they have black caps on their heads. They are medium-sized birds, weighing only around 4 ounces (113 g).

The Snowy Owl

The snowy owl is a large owl named for its snow-white feathers. Its feathers help it hide among the white landscape. While some snowy owls come to Alaska's tundra only in the summer, there are some that live there year-round.

The snowy owl is a great hunter. Snowy owls have sharp eyesight and great hearing, which helps them find **prey** that is under the snow. They also have specially-shaped feathers that allow them to fly without making any noise. This allows the owls to sneak up on their prey. Snowy owls hunt small mammals and other birds.

Snowy owls have yellow eyes and black bills. Female snowy owls, like the one shown here, are darker than male snowy owls.

Mosquitoes!

Just like other places in the world, Alaska's tundra has a lot of **insects** in the summer. **Mosquitoes**, for example, are common insects that are found when the weather turns warm. The puddles left by melting snow are excellent places for mosquitoes to mate, lay eggs, and have baby mosquitoes. Did you know that only female mosquitoes are bloodsuckers? Having a blood meal gives a female mosquito the power that she needs to lay her eggs.

Some of Alaska's tundra animals enjoy having many mosquitoes around. Mosquitoes are food for many birds and other insects that live in tundra.

This mosquito is shown holding on to a plant. Male mosquitoes do not feed on blood. Males feed on sweet matter found in plants, called nectar.

Freezing Fish

Fish are another part of a tundra habitat. The small arctic cod is a fish that lives in the seas that border Alaska's tundra. In ice-free water, you might see arctic cod swimming in schools, which are large groups of fish. In icy water, you might see arctic cod hiding in cracks in the ice.

Arctic cod live farther north than any other fish. The arctic cod can live in the tundra's icy waters because it has adapted in a special way. Arctic cod have matter in their blood that keeps the blood from freezing.

Here an arctic cod is shown swimming through the icy water off the tundra coast.

Saving Alaska's Tundra

Animals in Alaska's tundra have adapted to living in this climate. However, Alaska's tundra faces a climate change. Today, tundra climate is warmer than it was in the past. Harmful gases in the air have caused this change. A warmer climate causes ice and permafrost to melt, which has a bad effect on tundra animals. For example, the loss of sea ice leaves polar bears without a hunting ground.

People are working on slowing down climate change, though. Doing so will make sure that Alaska's tundra will be a living habitat for years to come.

Glossary

adapted (uh-DAPT-ed) Changed to fit requirements.

climate (KLY-mit) The kind of weather a certain place has.

frozen (FROH-zen) Hardened by great cold.

habitat (HA-beh-tat) The kind of land where animals or plants naturally live.

insects (IN-sekts) Small animals that often have six legs and wings.

mammals (MA-mulz) Animals that have a backbone and feed milk to their young.

mate (MAYT) To join together to make babies.

mosquitoes (muh-SKEE-tohz) Flying insects that feed on the blood of animals and the nectar of plants.

precipitation (preh-sih-pih-TAY-shun) Any water that falls from the sky.

prey (PRAY) An animal that is hunted by another animal for food.

roots (ROOTS) The parts of plants that grow underground.

temperature (TEM-pur-cher) How hot or cold something is.

Index

A
Alaska, 4, 14
arctic fox(es), 4, 12

C
climate(s), 4, 6, 10, 22
coat(s), 4, 10, 12

E
Earth, 6

F
feet, 4, 6, 12
fur, 4, 10

I
insects, 18

L
life, 4

M
mammals, 10, 12, 16

P
precipitation, 6, 8

R
roots, 8, 10

S
snow geese, 14
summer, 6, 10, 14, 16, 18

T
temperature, 6

U
United States, 4

W
weather, 14, 18
winter, 6, 8, 10, 12, 14
world, 4, 18

Web Sites

Due to the changing nature of Internet links, PowerKids Press has developed an online list of Web sites related to the subject of this book. This site is updated regularly. Please use this link to access the list:
www.powerkidslinks.com/amhab/tundra/